Parents are often surprised by the quality and the depth of their child's memory and observation, and many are beginning to recognise that the best time to learn is when everything is new and therefore important to the child.

Here is a series of six books designed to help parents to amuse, interest and at the same time to teach. *Shapes, Colours* and the Ladybird *abc* each have their part to play in bringing the child to an early understanding of the reading process; *Counting* teaches him to recognise and understand simple numbers, and *Telling the Time* shows him how to relate the time on a clock face to his everyday life. *Big and Little* deals with the words which describe relative sizes and positions, all shown through objects and scenes which will be familiar to the young child.

big and little

by HY MURDOCK

illustrated by SALLY LONG

Please return to
        E. Bartlet

Ladybird Books Loughborough

, Thank-you.

Things have different
shapes and sizes.

Some animals are **big**,
some animals are **little**.

Some people are **big**,

some are **middle-sized**

and some
are **little**.

Look at the lorries.
The blue one is **big**,
the red one is **bigger**,
but the green one is **biggest**.

All around us we see things which are **large** and **small**.

Here are some more shapes and sizes.

A **fat** clown

A **thin** clown

A **tall** policeman

A **short** policeman

A **long** dragon

A **short** dragon

The purple candle is big.

The blue
candle
is **small**.

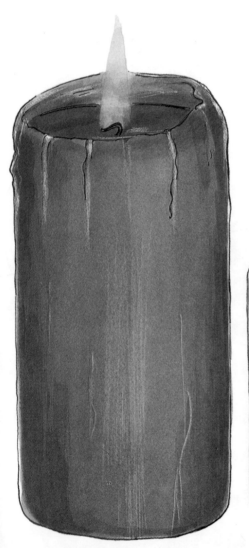

The red candle
is **smaller**.

The green candle
is **smallest**.

We find things in lots
of different positions.

The see-saw
goes **up**

and **down**.

The boy pushes
his bicycle
up the hill.

The girl rides
her bicycle
down the hill.

Have you seen an escalator?
Some people go **up**,

some people go **down**.

Incy Wincy spider
Climbing **up**
        the spout.
Down came the rain
And washed
        the spider out.
Out came the sun,
Dried up all the rain.
Incy Wincy spider,
Climbing **up** again.

The man paints
high up.

The little girl
paints **low**
down.

A **high** shelf

A **low** shelf

The balloon flies **high**,
the kite flies **higher**,
the aeroplane flies **highest**.

Humpty Dumpty sat **on** the wall

Humpty Dumpty fell **off** the wall

The television set is switched **on**.

The television set is switched **off**.

The boy has taken
his shoes and socks **off**.

The girl has her shoes and
socks **on**.

We put our clothes **on**
in the morning.

We take them **off** at bedtime.

Jack is
in the
box.

Jack is
out of the
box.

The red car is
in the car-wash
and the blue car
has come **out**.

The Easter egg has pretty paper on the **outside**.

The chocolate egg is **inside** the paper.

The children play
indoors

and **outdoors**.

The big blue candle is
in the middle of the cake.

The red candles are **round
the edge.**

The king is in the
middle.

The children dance **round**.

The books are **between**
the doll and the toy soldier.

The rabbit is at the **side**
of the bed.

The doll is on the **top** bunk.

The teddy is on the **bottom** bunk.

The car is **underneath** the bunk bed.

Talk about the picture . .

. . and make
up a story.